Lessons in Submissive Speech

Learning the Art of Speaking Submissively

Second Edition

Luna Carruthers
SubmissiveGuide.com

LESSONS IN SUBMISSIVE SPEECH

Copyright © 2019 by Luna Carruthers ALL RIGHTS RESERVED.

No part of this publication may be reproduced, distributed, or transmitted in any form or by any means, including photocopying, recording, or other electronic or mechanical methods, without prior written permission of the publisher, except in the case of brief quotations embodied in critical reviews and certain other noncommercial uses permitted by copyright law.

SubmissiveGuide.com

Cover, Cissi N. Hinderliter

Preface

In the world of D/s, there are many ways to do one thing or another – all of them considered correct and valid for the situation that they call for and the people involved. When it comes to speaking in a submissive way, there is nothing better than knowing your manners and having a variety of ideas to draw from to talk with respect and humility.

This book was put together to help you learn ways to present yourself as a humble and respectful person through your speech and word choice. It is not all submissive focused, and you can likely apply some of these lessons in your everyday life. It is by far not the only way to say things, and I do hope that you will take this information and customize it for your relationship or dynamic.

By the end of this book, you will learn the verbal skills to navigate several situations and experiences that could highlight your submissive demeanor or help to diffuse a difficult situation.

Contents

Preface..3
Contents...5
   Introduction to Submissive Speech................................9
What Is Submissive Speech?...11
   Guidelines for Polite Communication.............................14
   Don't Use That Tone With Me..19
Manners and Etiquette in Submissive Speech.......................27
   Asking a Question...28
   How to Apologize...32
   Responding or Answering in the Positive......................38
   Responding or Answering in the Negative....................41
   Showing Gratitude..45
   Topics to Avoid with Other Submissives........................48
Submissive Speech in Specific Situations.............................53
   Addressing Individuals..54
   Personal Introductions..58
   Polite Interruptions...63
   Answering the Phone or Door.......................................65

Speaking with Service Persons..70
Online Interaction..73
    How to Approach a Dominant You Are Interested In.................74
    How To Tell A Dominant That You Are Not Interested In Them
....77
    The Basics of Chat Room Etiquette..82
    Conclusion...89

Introduction to Submissive Speech

Not long after my first step into the world of BDSM, I learned of a phrase that to this day has no real definition that I can pin to it. That phrase is "submissive speech." To me, there is no way to speak submissively that is unique to submissives and isn't speaking respectfully and with deference. Other situations call for it, like in front of a judge or to their religious leaders.

But I still get questions about how a submissive is supposed to say x, y, and z so I thought that I'd do my best to convey what I think would work in a variety of circumstances so that if the occasion arises that you need to "speak submissively" you'll have some ideas of what you can say.

Every day there is a different reason or occasion for speaking in a submissive manner. From common exchanges to special events, there are moments where we're called upon to speak and show respect or submission with our words. With that in mind, this book should walk you through some of the situations where using the right words, tone of voice, or volume amplifies your submission and demonstrates humility in service. You'll learn how to answer the door, the phone, greet a Dominant, get someone's attention, and with respect and deference. I've also put together a section on online conversation which includes basic chat room etiquette, how to approach a Dominant, and how to decline a Dominant's interest.

As with everything I write, please take this information as one person's view on the topic. Your opinion may vary, and I'm thrilled that it might be. Even if that is the case, I imagine there is something from this book that you can add to your own submissive journey. These are only my ideas and experiences, and your personal training and skill sets may be different. Feel free to customize any of the suggestions to fit your needs.

Let's get started.

Chapter 1

What Is Submissive Speech?

What Is Submissive Speech?

When we talk about speaking submissively what we mean is that we approach communication from a mindset of respect, humility, compassion, and patience. It's a lot to expect out of an experienced submissive, let alone someone brand new.

But it can be learned. It should be discovered. If it's not expected of you all the time, at least you'll have it in your submissive arsenal for when an occasion might arise, say at a local play party or a regional BDSM convention.

There are a lot of things you can do to learn how to speak more respectfully. First, make sure you have a clear understanding of your Dominant on what they expect of your speech. As I mentioned above, the level of requirement is different for everyone and every occasion, so ask what sorts of demeanor or language is expected of you before you make any assumptions.

For example, my Dominant requires that I'm polite and that I call him Master in private when addressing him. I have unique phrases I am to say for specific situations, and I'm never to curse or raise my voice at him. Cursing is vulgar and only allowed during play and sex. I am to exhibit proper grammar and speak in a manner that is courteous and respectful at all times. These rules didn't just come about overnight. We've had years to add to and practice this level of speech protocol.

If you are better at writing to your Dominant than speaking, then work on thinking before you speak. There is no reason there can't be a pause before responding to questions or when you address your Dominant. I am still guilty of formulating a response before they're even finished speaking! Don't do this; it means you aren't actively listening to them and could miss something important.

At the beginning of my D/s relationship, I know I was a lot better at remembering to call him Master when I was writing to him at first, than when using it in speech. It was mostly because saying "Master" out loud felt odd. Of course, the only way for it to stop feeling odd is with practice. The more you say their title, the less uncomfortable you will feel about it.

Guidelines for Polite Communication

Polite speech is decided by where you're from and in what type of society you live. Gracious speech in one location may be rude in another. Some cultures have different meanings for polite behavior, and you have to be aware of those differences.

Interruptions

Generally speaking, interrupting is considered rude behavior. It shows that you don't respect the speaker or that you aren't listening to what they have to say. And if you're already formulating responses while the speaker is still talking, it's showing that you don't care what they are saying. Stop. Listen. Don't interrupt.

And if you absolutely need to interrupt, you will learn a respectful way to do so further in this book.

Non-verbal

You can also find respectful communication in your body language and facial expressions. When speaking, smiling can show that you are open and receptive. When listening, making eye contact is considered a polite way to show the speaker that you value what they say.

Keep in mind that nonverbal cues are not always reliable. Sometimes that frown you see on a listener's face is simply because they aren't feeling well, not that you said anything to cause it.

Considerations

Other ways politeness comes out as being considerate.

- Don't use your cell phone when you're in a check out line or supposed to be engaging with service persons.

- Don't let background noise interfere with your conversations.

What Is Submissive Speech?

- Don't assume familiarity with someone, use appropriate greetings and terms of address unless invited to do differently.

- Don't correct someone's grammar in front of others unless it is your name they mispronounce.

- Avoid conversations about others. Gossiping is considered rude.

You have to practice politeness to make it a part of your everyday speech. Use "please" every time you want something. Use thank you's once you've received something. "May I's" instead of "Can I's" and change statements like "I'm going to the store" to questions such as, "May I go to the store?"

Once you get a good grip on it, you won't even notice it. That is unless someone brings it to your attention. I often get complimented for being so polite to customer service people. I guess they just don't get treated well so when they do it gets noticed. It is a good thing to be noticed over.

The First Step is Silence

It may seem a bit odd, but the first step in learning about speaking submissively is ==learning when not to speak==. I feel in this modern age; we talk too much. We are always on our phones talking about useless, unimportant, happenstance things to stay connected with people. We are on social media taking pictures of the food we eat, the clothing we wear and the things we do. Every single minute of our day, we are talking or writing. It's a constant barrage of frivolous fluff. Our ears are so used to the noise that when we are faced with silence, it leaves us uncomfortable and trying to come up with anything to fill it.

Frequently the noises around us make it difficult to listen and in situations where listening is essential to understand any requests or general conversation from your Dominant it could make submission that much harder. ==Choose silence whenever you can==. If you have a meditation practice, which I suggest that you do, you will become accustomed to silence. Learn how to filter out all the background noise to focus on the task in front of you.

Practicing submissive speech is more about ==speaking when there is something of value to say==. Submissive speech is responding to the

What Is Submissive Speech?

situation, or the person you are serving. When sharing your daily rota, it is best to do so concisely without embellishment unless asked to do so. That isn't to say that you shouldn't speak unless spoken to if you don't have that requirement of you, but it is to say that you should be more aware of what you are saying and reduce the amount of "fluff" you are adding to your everyday.

Don't Use That Tone With Me

It is not always about the words we use but how we say things that speak a lot about our mood, impression of the situation, and so much more – our tone. The tone is also something precarious because you can be misunderstood by your tone alone. Written speech is worse because conveying mood is that much harder. How many times have you had to reiterate something because it was taken in a way that you didn't mean just by how you said it?

There are ways in which you can use a more submissive tone to your conversation and speech as a whole. Now, remember that this method isn't directly submissive but more along the lines of demure, with deference and humility. Everyone could learn to be a bit more appropriate from time to time. Here are a few tips that might help you be heard in the right perspective that you intended.

Learn Proper Pronunciation

The biggest reason that you may not be understood the way you intended is that your pronunciation is off. There are native stresses to every word in the English (and all other) language. If you speak correctly, then it's less likely that you will be misunderstood – unless that person hasn't learned the correct pronunciation either and it gets confusing for both speaker and listener. If you aren't sure about the pronunciation of words, then look up dictionary.com and listen to the pronunciation guides for words that seem to get misunderstood a lot.

Perhaps, for you, it may be inappropriate stresses that are causing the tone change.

Slurring words, over-abusing contractions, and using regional slang help to change the tone of conversation as well. A submissive should try to use proper pronounciation and grammar as often as possible. It not only shows intelligence but can bring your conversation to an even keel, keeping it humble.

Using Slang

There's more to slang than just using shortened terms, and depending on where you live and the social situations you're exposed to, such as prison, young teens and the internet, it can shift and change what you say to mean something completely different than intended.

While you may be comfortable using slang, you should try to limit its use when speaking to your Dominant or in any situation where complete understanding is necessary.

Keep Your Voice on an Even Level

When you emphasize words by making them louder than the rest of the sentence, it changes the tone of the entire conversation. The same goes for sudden whispers. Speaking evenly with the correct volume and pitch sounds calmer, more organized, and steady. Remaining calm when speaking shows a level of control that provides the listener with a relaxed interaction.

Be careful though, because having too much of a monotone voice can be just as poor and can give you an air of indifference, boredom

What Is Submissive Speech?

or laziness. You can have changes in pitch and volume without going through the roof with the shifts. You can learn to prevent your voice from being monotone with these tips:

1. Breathe. It's impossible to speak with power and presence if you have no breath behind it. If you are nervous, you may take shallow breaths, and that can lead to your voice losing its resonance. ==Find your calm before you speak.==

2. Stand up straight, don't slouch. You can't fill your lungs well if you're not sitting upright or standing straight. Yes, posture impacts your voice.

3. Pause. One common cause of monotony is never leaving any space between thoughts or words. Stop to breathe in-between sentences or when you switch thoughts. Slow down your speech. Silence isn't all bad and can help speak for you when necessary.

Use Less Commands and More Requests

In this rushed and harried day and age, we do far less asking and much more demanding than we ever used to do. "Give me this," "I want that," and "do this for me." It's all very commanding and not submissive-like. Are you in the habit of telling people what to do instead of asking? *yes*

It's not uncommon to think that Dominants like to give commands and submissives like to obey them, but it's not a common thing that happens. In my over 15 years of experience, I've heard and seen far more exchanges that involve requests other than commands. Can you think why?

We push back against being told what to do. I picture myself as a 7-year-old with the crossed arms and a stomping foot when I hear someone command me to do something or tell me how I should act.

I believe that we have an innate desire to help others. If I'm asked to do something I'll do almost anything.

What Is Submissive Speech?

Can you think of words that would convey a request rather than a demand?

- "May I... ?"

- "Could I... ?"

- "Would you... ?"

- =="Is it possible to... ?"==

We've all learned that it's so much easier to get things handled when you ask rather than demand. And the usual icing on the request is politeness. So say please and thank you!

Ask for Clarification

Often the change in tone in our voice is because we misunderstood what someone else said. If you aren't sure, ask for clarification. Or you can re-summarize what the person said before you respond.

Don't be a Loud Talker

This recommendation is for me, but I can't be the only one, so I'm sharing it here. I'm a loud talker. I often forget that the person is right in front of me and talk as if they are across the room. The tone this implies can be forceful, yelling, ignorance (on my part) and anger. Tone it down. Be heard. Use that inside voice.

What Is Submissive Speech?

Chapter 2

Manners and Etiquette in Submissive Speech

Asking a Question

It is my personal belief that you should never be afraid to ask a question of your Dominant, however, in certain circumstances, there are inappropriate times for questioning, inappropriate ways to ask questions and inappropriate questions.

First, you shouldn't question a Dominant's orders. It is not a submissive's position to know why a Dominant wishes something done or the reason behind it. As hard as it may seem, we should just do it and trust our Dominant with that decision.

However, with exceptions to every rule, there are instances where a submissive should question a Dominant's request. You should challenge the Dominant:

Lessons in Submissive Speech

- When the new request contradicts a previous one.

- When a request puts the Dominant, submissive or someone else at risk.

- When a command is illegal or may have legal repercussions.

- When an order violates the verbal or written contract negotiations within the relationship.

A submissive should always ask questions to clarify a request of the Dominant so that the order can be carried out correctly. There is no excuse for a job done poorly if you know precisely what is expected of you. You should not fear to ask these types of questions.

Typical questions in lower protocol situations:

- "Is there anything I can get you, Sir?"

- "May I be excused to use the facilities, Ma'am?"

Manners and Etiquette in Submissive Speech

- "How would you like your steak prepared tonight, Master?"

- "Could you clarify what you mean by scrub the floor properly, Sir?"

In more formal relationships or situations, it may be proper for a submissive to ask if they may ask a question. In these situations, it is common to ask, "May I ask a question/ask for clarification, Sir?"

These more formal relationships often also have a particular way that questions need to be formulated. They should be concise and to the point without a lot of extra chatter. Formal questions always begin with an apology.

- "Pardon me..."

- "Excuse me..."

- "My apologies..."

- "I am sorry, Sir..."

As with all excellent communication, if you need clarification, you can rephrase the Dominant's request or ask for specific clarification on points mentioned.

Asking too many questions is a sign of inexperience or lack of confidence in your abilities. However, it is always favorable to ask questions than to make a mistake because you did not understand the request.

Manners and Etiquette in Submissive Speech

How to Apologize

The proper apology is an art, it really is. But before we put that together, I'd like to cover the reason for apologizing in the first place.

Apologizing is not admitting your intentional disobedience. It's not about accepting the blame either. It is purely about acknowledging that you have displeased your Dominant in some way; it's about knowing that your Dominant is unhappy and that you will take every step to make sure it does not happen again.

I've made this mistake I don't know how many times in the past, thinking that if I apologized that I'd be accepting the blame or that I misstepped on purpose. I'm still learning this hard truth, so I hope that by sharing it with you here it will give you some pause to think of your own situations. Don't refuse to apologize – that is direct disobedience. Take it upon yourself to correct your Dominant's displeasure with an apology. Then move on.

Nothing is worse than being on the receiving end of an apology that sounds more like it's a backhanded wave of secondary attacks, and the last thing that you want to do is turn your apologetic conversation into a battlefield; so before you apologize, keep these things in mind:

1. Know why you're apologizing. Know what you did or said, understand why it was wrong, and know what you could have done or said differently.

2. Understand before you apologize that an apology doesn't equate automatic forgiveness. We all hope that our apologies are accepted—especially when those apologies are sincere—but understand that an apology might not make someone feel better right away. Consider your impending apology the start to making things better.

3. Approach the person when you're both in a better mindset. You need to be able to think clearly and rationally, and they need to be able to concentrate on what you're saying. Give both of you the respect of being in a calm environment and in a situation where you can both dedicate time and concentration to the conversation.

Manners and Etiquette in Submissive Speech

4. Forget about your personal motivations. The conversation where you apologize for your actions is not the conversation where you should be offering excuses for why the person you're apologizing to shouldn't be mad at you. If you're apologizing, it doesn't matter why you said or did what you said or did, and it's bad form to push a justification onto the person you're apologizing. Don't allude to whether you had a reason or not, and don't offer the reason unless the person who you're apologizing to wants to know.

A casual apology is always, "I'm sorry" or "Pardon me" or "I apologize." It is enough for most Dominants for small infractions and slips of behavior.

A Formal Apology

A simple apology may not be all that is needed. Sometimes the problem is something that extends past the D/s dynamic or the infraction is more monumental to your relationship. A more extensive apology may be necessary.

Lessons in Submissive Speech

There are **four steps to a formal proper apology.** I'm sorry is not enough. It's never enough. It is the starting point, though.

You **initiate the apology** with a phrase along these lines.

- "I'm sorry..."

- "Please forgive me..."

- "I apologize..."

- "I beg your pardon..."

Then you **give an acclimation** where you admit the error or offense. If you do not know what you did wrong, you can still admit to a mistake.

- "I was unaware your cup was empty."

- "It was not my intention to displease you."

- "I missed your first set of directions."

Manners and Etiquette in Submissive Speech

Next, you **provide an affirmation** that will assure the Dominant that you intend for it to not happen in the future.

- "I assure you this will not happen again."

- "I will make every effort to be more aware of your needs."

- "I will see that it never happens again."

And then finally you **present an offer of acceptance** which could be for punishment or immediate correction of your misdeed.

- "I present myself for your correction so that I may remember this incident."

- "Please allow me to refresh your beverage."

- "May I do anything to correct my mistake now, Sir?"

My formal personal apology for my misbehavior to KnyghtMare is:

"I'm sorry, Master, I was a bad girl, it won't happen again, please forgive me." I have to say that no matter where I am or what I'm doing if I am found to have made a mistake. It's hard in public, trust me. But I think that's part of the chastisement – that I have to say it in public.

Lastly, you have to feel sorry. Just saying the words will not correct the mistake. You have to feel it and remember it and make sure it is fixed for the future. Now, I'm not saying you have to remind yourself of your slips continually, but be more aware. Learn from these tips, and you can lessen the need to have to apologize in the first place.

Responding or Answering in the Positive

Saying yes is one of the most frequent phrases I say regularly. When I first started exploring submission, I thought that was the only appropriate response to anything asked of me. Nowadays I know to give it a bit of thought before I respond affirmatively, but in practically all cases, a "yes" response suffices.

When a submissive says "yes" it can be as simple or elaborate as the Dominant wishes. How it is said depends on the level of protocol and the explicitness of the request for the submissive.

Here are some ideas for how you can answer positively in a D/s context.

For example, if your Dominant asked you, "are you thirsty?" here are a few ways you could answer with a "yes":

Lessons in Submissive Speech

- "Yes, Sir."

- "This slave would gratefully accept something to drink Master."

- "Sir, yes, Sir."

- "Yes, please, I am thirsty. May I have something to drink?"

- "I am thirsty Sir, thank you for caring for me."

Other affirmative responses:

- "With pleasure, Sir."

- "I'd be happy to do that for you, Sir."

- "If you wish it, Master."

Answering in the affirmative may not require speech at all. In a relaxed environment or when speaking would interrupt, a nod of the head and a look at the Dominant may be enough to convey your positive acknowledgment.

Affirmative Response But With Questions

Sometimes you might have questions related to the request you just received. We all want to excel at the task just given to us, and want to do it precisely as the Dominant would like, so making sure the job is clear before setting out is vital.

When you need to ask questions but have no problem performing as long as those questions are cleared up, say your "yes" response first. Then follow up with your questions. Saying yes first will show your partner that you will do it but need some further direction. Dominants are not mind readers, and neither are you, so if you aren't sure how to do the task if you don't have all the information you need, make sure you get it.

Remember that slang is not welcome in a submissives speech set in most cases, so words like "yeah," "yup," and "uh-huh" should be avoided and considered inappropriate unless that is the Dominant's preference. In a more formal structured relationship, the words "sure," and "okay" could also be banned from an acceptable affirmative response.

Responding or Answering in the Negative

Just as saying yes or answering in the affirmative can be said many ways, saying no has many ways you can say it too.

When a submissive gives a negative answer, it can be a simple "no," or it can be as elaborate as the Dominant wishes. Some Dominants do not allow the submissive to use the word "no" at all. In my experience with my Dominant, if I say no that I had better have a good reason for it. So, perhaps you have to explain why you are saying no with your negative response.

If you think that saying "no" would be more like, "not until I have more information," then refer back to Answering in the Affirmative with Questions.

Manners and Etiquette in Submissive Speech

This book isn't going to argue whether submissives or slaves have a right to say no, or if saying no is a form of topping from the bottom. We're just dealing with when saying no is necessary.

Here are some ideas for how you can answer negatively in a D/s context depending on preference and situation.

For example, if the Dominant asked, "Are you warm?":

- "This slave is not warm, Master."

- "Sir, no, Sir."

- "No Master, I am not warm Master, thank you for caring for me."

- "Not unless you wish it, Sir."

- "I am not warm, Master."

- "No, thank you, Ma'am."

- "Not at this time, Sir."

- "No Mistress."

Verbalizing may not be necessary at all. A simple downcast of the eyes and a shake of the head to indicate a negative response always works.

When You Say No: Attitude, Judgment, and Alternatives

When you are submissive, the moments when saying no is necessary may be for a variety of reasons, but there are things to keep in mind as you formulate your negative response.

Try to avoid having a bad attitude about it. You may not have agreed to the request, and perhaps the topic is something that doesn't work for you for whatever reason, this isn't the moment for attitude. You are still submissive, and you are still trying to maintain that mindset through this without throwing disrespect.

Manners and Etiquette in Submissive Speech

Along with zipping up that attitude, don't express judgment for what you're being asked to do. Criticism for their desires, self-righteousness or personal opinion have no room in the moment of saying no. If it crosses a line or a limit you are adamant not be crossed then say so, but keep your mind on your position and do your best not to make them feel lesser for asking it.

One way to help you keep your attitude and criticism at bay is to offer up alternatives that you could do that might fill the same purpose that they were desiring. After all, sometimes it's not saying no if you can suggest something that would be equally appealing. Be prepared for your Dominant not to accept your suggestions, though. If your partner would prefer to make all the decisions and your adding in ideas isn't going to be welcome, you could simply phrase it something like this:

"I'm sorry, Sir, I can't do what you ask because [insert reason here], but perhaps we can come up with something else to do instead?"

As with affirmative responses, it is essential to remember that casual slang like "nope," "nah," and "nuh-uh" should be avoided and considered inappropriate unless that is the preference of the Dominant.

Showing Gratitude

One of the most valuable things that I think any submissive should know is how to express gratitude in more than one way. I know I've taken a lot for granted when I was new and exploring kink with anyone interested. Never once did I say thank you for it. I was an ungrateful submissive.

I'm not perfect now, but I know more about saying thank you and the value that it can have. Take the following steps to make your gratitude come from the heart. Use it well and use it often.

1. Take the time to comprehend that gratitude comes from within. Understand that gratitude is a reflection and perspective; therefore, it's difficult to extend it to anyone unless one starts practicing it as a way of life.

2. Select a modest and sincere wording without overwhelming the person who did a good deed. Don't make it sound flimsy and

lazy with something that had a severe impact on your life or well-being.

3. Service personnel makes it their job to make sure you are happy and pleased with their service. Do your best to show your appreciation as often as possible. Don't take their service for granted.

Being thankful can take on many forms, and each time we feel that sensation of gratitude well up, we can use a different display of appreciation. For example, thanking your Dominant for giving you an orgasm will be treated differently than if you are grateful that they hold power in your submissive life. Orgasm gratitude is usually expressed immediately after while you may take a while to express your feelings for the latter.

Taking what I've shared above, what are some excellent ways to say thank you? Here are a few suggestions to get you started.

- "Thank you kindly for allowing me to sit next to you."

- "I appreciate the hard work you do when we play together."

- "This girl is grateful for the generosity you have shown her."

- "Thank you very much!"

How do you say thank you?

Manners and Etiquette in Submissive Speech

Topics to Avoid with Other Submissives

If you get two submissives in a room together, a discussion will likely take place about their Dominant partners. We sure love to talk about them, don't we?

I can't tell you how many times I've talked about KnyghtMare at the local submissive forum. It's usually with pride and love that he comes to the forefront of discussion. He has guidelines for what I'm allowed to talk about when it comes to my talking with other people, probably because I talk about him so frequently. It makes good common sense.

Throughout this book, we've learned about some of the ways we can be courteous and respectful and show deference when we speak, but now I want to talk about knowing when not to say anything. Some topics are inappropriate that we should respect even in our BDSM circles.

Lessons in Submissive Speech

Gossip is a negative breeding ground for strife and drama. It's unnecessary and awful for a group or social situation. If you gossip or are prone to be gossiped to, make today the day you stop it in its tracks. A phrase that I have said on many occasions when gossip starts around me, I'd like to share with you also, "I don't think we should be talking about someone who can't defend themselves." I've also had to tell someone, "I'm not into gossip."

Sure, if it means people talk to me less about the "did you hear" and "guess what happened" then that's fine. Below is a list of topics that I feel you shouldn't talk about with other submissives when it comes to our partners and our relationships.

- Never speak ill of your Dominant, unless there are legal issues or the submissive is in physical danger.

- Never speak ill of another submissive's Dominant, if you see something inappropriate, go directly to your partner and talk with him or her.

- Never discuss your Dominant's finances or lack thereof.

- Never make fun of your Dominant.

Manners and Etiquette in Submissive Speech

- Never discuss your Dominant as such with anyone outside the lifestyle.

- Never discuss anything that will embarrass or dishonor your Dominant.

Competition

Competition is human nature. From the time we are children, we start to see who is 'better' and hopefully, that is you. It could be as simple as having more ice cream than your sibling, thus making you better or getting the best grade on a test, making you better than everyone else in the class. We have all compared ourselves with others; sometimes we 'win,' sometimes we 'lose.' It is when we voice these opinions out loud that we might not realize the ramifications.

On a forum recently, a submissive was explaining her life and how she struggled with something. Someone commented that they must not be submissive enough and that opened the gateway for competition. From people saying that they wouldn't behave that way, or a good submissive would do this or that it's all saying (even if it might not be true) that I'm better than you are because I know the answer. As if there were just one answer.

There is no such thing as not submissive enough.
Submissives are as different as snowflakes. Telling someone that they aren't submissive enough is just a means to belittle them and is not appropriate for any submissive to do. What I try to convey on Submissive Guide is that there is a proper way to act and behave. That is with common courtesy and manners. How would you feel if someone told you that you weren't skinny enough or sexy enough or feminine/masculine enough?

Unless you are willing to put yourself up on the box to have your submission picked apart, keep it to yourself. It's not doing anyone any good.

Your relationship isn't better than theirs, just different.

Those of us lucky enough to live in our submission full time are not better than those who get to do it in bits and pieces. Submissives come from all walks of life and look for relationships to fill individual needs. It could be that they are looking for a full-time D/s relationship, and it could be that they aren't. Telling someone that their relationship isn't D/s enough or judging them based on how frequently they play is just childish and rude.

Try not to compare your life with someone else's. In the end, you will fail to see the point of their discussion because you will be too busy finding the flaws in their relationship that don't make it just like yours. Be thankful you are in a relationship.

Chapter 3

Submissive Speech in Specific Situations

Addressing Individuals

Submissives in BDSM commonly have to learn how to address someone in a non-scene scenario. How many times have you had conversations with service personnel or with people you encounter in your day to day without first asking them their names or how they wish to be addressed? It's a silent understanding that if they offer you their name they want you to use it and if they don't, then you use personal pronouns instead.

But in a more formal social environment where BDSM individuals gather, we all start concerning ourselves with knowing how someone prefers to be addressed, and we do our best not to offend anyone by using those addresses frequently.

Especially when you are a submissive or slave where a level of protocol is expected, that's the key here, if there's no agreed protocol then don't make assumptions that protocol is required. In most situations, common courtesy is the best way to start.

You may also learn that certain people want to be called with gender-neutral pronouns or with pronouns different than what they may appear.

Addressing Superiors

Each Dominant has a preference for how they wish to be addressed. Some will allow submissives to use their first name, and others will request you use Mr. or Mrs and still others will ask for polite courtesy and the use of Sir or Ma'am. How they'd prefer to be addressed can also depend on how well you know the Dominant.

A submissive should never assume that they know how a Dominant wishes to be addressed. There are many ways you can ask them politely, for example:

- "Pardon me, but I do not know how you wish to be addressed."

- "Please excuse me, but I am unaware of how you like to be addressed."

Submissive Speech in Specific Situations

- "I apologize, I am unfamiliar with the way that you wish to be addressed."

- "Hello, I'm Luna, nice to meet you. What's your name?"

If you are in a situation where you can not ask, such as if there are people nearby that are not in the lifestyle then Sir and Ma'am are almost always okay as it's common courtesy until told to do otherwise.

Addressing Equals

It's normal for us submissives and slaves to seek out people that we can befriend and get support. The most important thing to remember is that even in these instances, your behavior reflects on your Dominant and yourself.

A submissive should try to treat other individuals as superiors until permitted to do otherwise. This also includes other submissives and slaves.

It is common courtesy when addressing someone that you don't know, to assume that they are superior to you until known otherwise. You should ask them how they prefer to be addressed just as in the "addressing superiors" section above.

When in an environment of mixed company, the use of honorifics like Miss and Sir are acceptable and welcome.

Once you know them, submissives and slaves are often called by their names. They're on your level after all, and some may become close friends.

Addressing Subordinates

It is likely that as a submissive there are very few people below you on the totem pole. First, you should know how your Dominant requires that you address people of equal or lower station.

Remember, no one will ever fault a submissive for having too good of manners, only if they are lacking in some way.

Submissive Speech in Specific Situations

Personal Introductions

Generally speaking, the first time you encounter someone in a BDSM context, you will likely have to introduce yourself. We've all heard that you only get one chance to make a first impression, so make sure it's a good one.

I'm going to break this up into two separate sections. One for single submissives and situations that are casual or low protocol and then the other part will be a higher protocol situation. Use what works best for you and make sure you talk about all this with your partner before adopting anything.

Greeting a Dominant that you do not know with a title they didn't earn shows a sign of ignorance or an untrained submissive. You should never approach someone with "Hello Master" or "Greetings Mistress." It's inappropriate and will get you discarded as someone who has skimmed too many BDSM fantasy novels.

Lessons in Submissive Speech

Also, if you get an introduction from a Dominant and they say you have to call them by a title that you are uncomfortable with, this is a sign of an ignorant or novice Dominant. Sir and Ma'am are almost always okay as it's common courtesy. But even that is a bit much in low or no protocol situations. Often, scene names are plenty.

Speaking of scene names, pick one that you're comfortable using to introduce yourself. There are social media accounts with some pretty insane usernames, and if I heard someone introduce themselves as Princess Titty Jiggler or WellHung9Inch, I'd probably roll my eyes.

You may want to ask a person how they'd like to be addressed before you introduce yourself. It's usually good form around people you know to be Dominants but can work for anyone.

1. "Pardon me, but I do not know how you wish to be addressed."

2. "Please excuse me, but I am unaware of how you like to be addressed."

Remember to thank them for sharing their preferred address before your introduction.

Submissive Speech in Specific Situations

Casual and Low Protocol Introductions

Since relaxed atmospheres are more common for BDSM socials, these suggestions will likely always work for you. The phrases can also come easier to you because they feel more natural. Once you know how to address the person, your introduction could go something like these.

- "Hello Sir, I'm luna nice to meet you."

- "I don't believe we have met before Ms. Joy. I'm luna, submissive to KnyghtMare."

- "I'm so happy to make your acquaintance George. My name is luna, and I belong to KnyghtMare."

Another way introductions happen in BDSM social settings is the introduction period where everyone stands up and introduces themselves individually. It's not as common as mingling and doing individual introductions, but you should be prepared if this situation arises.

Lessons in Submissive Speech

A good introduction to the group does not have to go into your life story. Include your name, if your local or from out of town and if you identify as Dominant, submissive, switch, slave or some other role.

- "Hello, I'm luna. I'm submissive to KnyghtMare, and we're from Central City."

- "Hello, everyone. My name is luna. This is my first social, so I'm rather nervous. I don't know if I'm Dominant or submissive, and I traveled an hour to get here tonight."

High Protocol Introductions

Higher protocol requires for a more formal way to introduce yourself. High protocol events are rare but declare themselves as such before you'd attend, so you know what sort of interaction to expect. A higher protocol has a level of amplified courtesy, and in many cases, the submissives are not allowed to speak unless spoken to. Being a representation of the Dominant's training is vital.

Submissive Speech in Specific Situations

Don't forget to obtain the preferred way to be addressed before introducing yourself.

- "If it pleases you, Sir, I am called luna."

- "It is an honor to meet you, Ms. Joy. I am called luna, submissive to KnyghtMare."

- "It is an honor to make your acquaintance George. If I may, I am luna, submissive to KnyghtMare."

Keep in mind that good manners are always expected.

Polite Interruptions

In everyone's daily exchanges with people, there comes a time we will need to interrupt another person or persons to pass on information. For a polite and graceful submissive, you should endeavor not to interrupt someone needlessly but to find an appropriate time to step into their presence. Often I am sent as a messenger for my Dominant and have to interrupt someone to pass on a message.

A few useful phrases to have on hand for this purpose are:

- "Pardon me."

- "Excuse me."

- "I don't mean to intrude."

Submissive Speech in Specific Situations

- "May I have a moment of your time?"

- "This one has a message from Sir Dom, may I proceed?"

- "I humbly beg your pardon for my intrusion."

If you wish to speak to someone that is in a conversation with someone else, approach them but to not enter their sphere (the invisible bubble that people make around themselves) and wait until you are acknowledged. You may go into a resting pose, otherwise waiting with hands at your sides in an unassuming manner always looks best. Do not concern yourself with their conversation, and it is rude to eavesdrop. Once acknowledged, then you may use one of the useful phrases above and pass on the information.

If you do interrupt someone unintentionally then apologize immediately and quickly so that they may continue with what they deem to be most important to them at the time. Of course, as you might imagine, not interrupting someone at all is the best and most polite thing to do.

Answering the Phone or Door

Sometimes we forget that speaking in a submissive manner could include moments we don't know who is on the other end of the conversation. Answering the phone or the door is a process that has gotten far too sloppy lately. I hope that with this advice we can begin to correct that. At least in our homes. We'll cover formal and informal ways to answer the phone and the door. Practice makes perfect but also be sure to be sincere in your delivery. No one likes a bored, frustrated, or irate-sounding greeting.

Answering the Phone

Phone greetings need to be three things; helpful, sincere, and simple. I know we've all been on the other end of a phone greeting that went on so long that you wondered if the person was ever going

Submissive Speech in Specific Situations

to stop trying to sell you their latest deal so that you could ask them what their hours were. Depending on the level of protocol in your relationship, you could use formal or informal phone greetings.

- "Hello, Smith residence, Jane speaking."

- "Good day, this is the Smith residence, I'm Jane. May I help you?"

Formal Greetings

Formal greetings traditionally have a greeting, an identification of the person answering the phone and an offer to serve. You can likely find a personal and relaxed way of doing this in your own home.

Informal Greetings

With the invention of caller ID, we have gotten lazy with answering the phone informally. It is jarring to have the person answer with their name, such as "Hi Jane! I'm so glad you called!" even before they got a breath to speak. Allow them the courtesy you would afford someone you don't know on the line and say "hello?" first.

Everyone knows how to answer the phone informally but to remind you, try to use full words. Avoid slang, speaking too quickly or with uncommon greetings. I've been greeted with "Yo!", "Go!" "What?!" and "Hiya" before. That does not convey the appropriate etiquette for a phone conversation – even if you know who is on the other line.

Answering the Door

I'll admit I don't get a lot of visitors to my home. Those that do visit have to go through a call box at the front door, so I use a phone answering informal greeting until they get to the door. In which case I know who is coming to my door.

But that isn't always the case for everyone, and you need to present yourself courteously to visitors who come to your door.

Submissive Speech in Specific Situations

First, if you are a cautious person and wish to know who it is before you open the door, then you need the visitor to announce themselves. Even if you have a peephole, this might be necessary. Speaking through the door is possible in most cases and isn't considered rude, as long as it is a short, simple exchange.

"Hello? Who is it?"

Once it has been decided that you are going to open the door, you need to do so with confidence, not caution. Don't hide behind the door. You are the first person they see, and you still represent your Dominant in your mannerisms.

- "Welcome to the Smith residence. How may I help you?"

- "Hello, I'm Jane, what brings you to our home?"

Once you have greeted them, if you have the intention, and perhaps permission to allow them inside, step aside so that they may step into your home. Each person has a comfort level for how far visitors are welcome, and your moving aside will display that personal bubble to them.

Remember to be polite and respectful. Even unknown visitors deserve a sincere greeting and treated with respect. That includes the occasional faith representatives and scouts selling goods.

Speaking with Service Persons

Think about the last time you went out to eat or stood in line at a check-out counter. Do you remember looking at the service person who waited on you? Did you smile at them and greet them, or did you stay on your cell phone and not even acknowledge them as they served you?

We've grown rude and detestable with how we treat the service personnel that we encounter daily. With shame, I admit that I too used to treat them as less than me, and not worth even the most common courtesy as a smile in greeting.

But not long after I met KnyghtMare, he corrected that. First, he insisted that I be the go-between for service persons and himself. This required that I engage them more than I had done in the past. Doing this, I learned valuable lessons about how my treatment of others impacted my service to him.

Lessons in Submissive Speech

You may be wondering why this subject is in a series on speaking submissively, but a considerable part of speaking submissively is courtesy and respect. We can learn a lot about how we treat our intimate relationships but seeing how we treat the people we interact with daily.

How to Show Respect to Service Persons

- Stay off the phone. Don't text or talk while being served by someone. Tell the person on the other end that you will call them back. Make a face to face exchange the most important.

- Look the person in the eye. Smile and talk to them, not at them. Make a note of what they look like so that you can find them later if you need to. (How many times have you asked others in your party what your server looks like? No more!)

- If they introduce themselves with their name, use it. "Hello, I'm Jane, and I'll be your server tonight." "Hello Jane, what are your drink specials?" "Jane, could I get some more coffee, please?"

Submissive Speech in Specific Situations

"Thank you, Jane." It makes the exchange more personal, and they will remember you as being courteous. This tip also works if they wear a name tag, but can be more jarring to the service person because they forget they are wearing their name on their chest. A thank you is decent enough and rarely causes a huge shock but more of a welcoming smile.

- Be polite. Use those manners you know you have. It makes every situation go by smoother and more comfortable.

- Don't yell. Even if you are angry, you aren't mad at the person, but the situation. Getting what you want to be resolved will be a lot easier if you remember that the person trying to help you didn't cause the condition.

What other ways do you know to show respect and courtesy to service persons?

Chapter 4

Online Interaction

Online Interaction

How to Approach a Dominant You Are Interested In

With online contact, you are likely on a dating site or social network, and I'm going to assume that for this part of the book. My rule here is straightforward: keep your first email very short. Give anything longer than three sentences a good, hard look before sending.

There are a few reasons why I feel short emails work best:

- Your profile is what you should be using to get people interested in you, not your first email. It should hold enough for someone to make a decision about communicating with you. If it doesn't, don't try and fix it in your emails: go back to your profile and improve that first. The email should be the bait to get someone to view your profile.

- If they don't like your profile, a long email isn't going to change their mind.

- You have to keep your weird factor low. People get emails from psychos all the time; I'm sure you've received some as well. Remember you are battling all the wrong impressions from people who have come before you.

First, try to include something that proves you've read their profile. People appreciate that you've taken the time to look at their profile, just as you are hoping that they will do the same to yours.

Second, if you find something of interest or in common from their profile, then mention that area in your message. (If there is more than one, just mention one.)

Finally, I suggest you ask them a question. You want to try and engage them in conversation, are you not?

Online Interaction

Most emotion is lost in online communication (and anyone who has used a :) in emails agrees with me). To avoid this, I would try to show my true level of interest by exaggerating it. Also, I feel that making someone feel "liked" early on would help them feel more comfortable and more likely to respond.

How To Tell A Dominant That You Are Not Interested In Them

Imagine this. You are bombarded with private messages from every Dominant in a 500-mile radius offering their control for your submission, usually only of the sexual kind. They send you penis pictures and say they are a true Master with two-times the years' experience than they are old.

Not hard to imagine? You mean you are one of the afflicted? No way!

Often these people are very fake, only looking for some kinky sex or a weekend of rough sex. Other times they could be dangerous predators looking for their next victim. Even if they are honest applications for your consideration, you will find that most of them you will be turning down or ignoring altogether. How can you turn

Online Interaction

someone down and keep your strength and honesty in-tact? How can you let them down respectfully?

Okay so some of you are thinking, why would you bother with courtesies anyway? I'm going to tell you that you need to be a better person. You need to treat them as you wish to be treated even if they don't reciprocate. Let me be clear. I'm hoping you'll learn to be a positive influence in your own life and have as few regrets as possible. Treating someone poorly when a little sugar does the same thing is not a very decent thing to do and not something a prospective or current partner would want.

How To Graciously Tell Them to Go Away Online

When the message is online, and you don't want to be too hurtful, but you do want them to get the hint that you are not interested in them, a short and quick reply should do the trick. In most cases, you may get a response that will be as gracious as you were, but in other times you will get the desperate whiners that you wouldn't want to speak with anyhow.

> Hello DOM,
>
> Thank you for contacting me. Unfortunately, I am not interested in conversing with you.
>
> —sub

Another method and one that I have done myself is to have a stock response that I save in a file and then copy and paste it to the person. Feel free to use this and alter it to fit your style if you like.

Online Interaction

Hello DOM,

Thank you, kindly for contacting me. However, I am not interested in kindling a relationship with you. The reason can be one of many, but the following tend to apply in most cases.

- I am in a happy, committed relationship and am not looking for another.

- You only talk of sex and kink you wish to participate in. I like the whole picture.

- I do not carry relationships online.

- I am offended by your use of your penis as a profile picture.

- Your interests do not mesh with mine.

- You are not single.

- You are not within my preferred age, body type, or gender.

- You live too far away.

- You chose not to use proper spelling and grammar in your message.

Thank you for your time,

—sub

Online Interaction

The Basics of Chat Room Etiquette

If you've never been in a chat room before, let alone a chat room with a BDSM slant, then you may be entering a whole other world and with that - the rules and etiquette are foreign to you. Just as with every new experience you learn as you go, but I'm going to share with you some of the more basic and general rules that chat rooms tend to have. Make sure you ask when you enter if there are any special rules you need to follow.

Be respectful and treat everyone kindly. Whether you are there for a chat or cyber relationships, everyone deserves respect online.

DON'T TALK IN CAPITAL LETTERS! In the online world, it is seen as shouting and is rude.

Don't idle. Engage in conversation. If you are new and not sure what to say, ask if it's okay to watch for awhile.

Be patient with others. They may be carrying on more than one conversation, can't type fast or have interruptions away from the computer. Chat conversation is slow-paced.

Don't private message anyone without first acquiring permission in open chat. People hold their private messages as an invasion of privacy if you intrude with them.

Let the administrators of the chat room do their job. You are not there to police anyone but yourself. If you see rule violations, alert the admin and then move on.

It is common in D/s chat rooms that submissives who have a Dominant to wear an online collar. Online only relationships are indicated with initials inside curly brackets, for example, luna{KM}. Real-time relationships are often noted with initials inside square brackets, like this: luna[KM]. This is not always the case, so if you see a name and aren't sure, then ask.

Hopefully, you feel more comfortable branching into online/cyber chat rooms with this information. There is a variety of them online; Submissive Guide has its own Discord Chat.

Online Interaction

Join the Submissive Guide Discord : https://discord.gg/rbqYJQd

Common Speech Protocols Online

I was once an online submissive. I know a bit about the language and grammar rules that reside there. They are creative and interesting and serve their purpose online. When you bring them into real life, they get more annoying, but in some relationships and dynamics, they still serve their purpose. What language adjustments am I talking about? Well, there's slash speak, third person and capped/uncapped.

Slash Speak

Slash Speak is when S/someone uses capital and regular case letters whenever Y/you use a pronoun or person identifying a word that could include Dominants and submissives. It is used only in written speech online and for the R/reader can get very confusing very quickly. I tend to avoid reading it if at all possible. It wasn't always the case because it's trendy in online chat rooms. It's supposed to show submission in that Y/you recognize there are Dominants and submissives present or could be accounted for in Y/your conversation. What's interesting is how many Dominants I've seen use this form of writing as well. (I exaggerated the slash speak in this paragraph.)

Third Person

Very popular in the Gorean IRC channels, the third person is when the slave/submissive is not allowed to refer to themselves in the 1st person. I believe it is used to enhance the role of the slave into believing that they are nothing more than property and are granted no personal power by removing their identity. One of my favorite bloggers and a contributor on SubmissiveGuide, thisgirl, used to use this form of writing on her blog by choice.

Online Interaction

Capped/Uncapped

I tend to still follow this form of writing even on Submissive Guide. If you'll notice I tend to capitalize Dominant, Owner, Master, Mistress and other titles for the Top side of the D/s equation. I guess it started on IRC, but it's one that I find the least annoying and I haven't had a single person say that it makes what I write hard to read, so I continue doing it. It also follows that I will get lowercase submissive titles, as well as names if that is how they are shared with me. I am luna, not Luna, although I will never correct someone because I don't force anyone to follow my personal protocol in that regard. It also means if you introduce yourself as Slave, I will not change it and call you a slave. I respect you enough to not force my personal protocol for you.

But what other language rules exist in BDSM dynamics? You name it, then it probably exists. I'm not allowed to curse except during sex and playtime and still within that I really shouldn't call my Owner names because he doesn't like it. I can't call him by his first name in most situations. We have alternatives that work for me to remember that I am deferring to him.

I'm only mildly familiar with silence rules, where submissives are restricted from talking at all for periods. Or with the interesting way to speak where you have to say Master before and after EACH sentence. But in every situation, they seem to serve a purpose.

In all situations, altering speech and writing is to do an important task of reminding the person that they are not in control of themselves, which includes their speech. They are asked to use deference in situations that call for it and even to learn a new way to talk to keep them in a submissive role. It is not expected that you will be asked to use any of these speech changes. Every Dominant is different.

Every submissive is different too. Make sure you know and can express in negotiations if you are comfortable with having these speech changes applied to you.

Online Interaction

Conclusion

As you've read, there are many ways you can incorporate a more submissive-like speech to almost any situation, and frequently, the case may be not to speak at all. I don't expect you to walk away from this and instantly be able to use all of these new ideas in your everyday conversations, but hopefully, you'll have a better understanding when someone says that there was a more submissive or better way to phrase something.

I am far from perfect, and I'm okay with that. I learned a lot from putting this book together, and I hope that you picked up a few things too. You can always find interesting knowledge and opinions on my website, Submissive Guide (https://submissiveguide.com). I hope to see you there.

About lunaKM

Luna Carruthers has been a submissive since 2004. She has been in leadership of several local BDSM communities and has presented on topics about D/s dynamics and BDSM. In 2009, she started SubmissiveGuide.com, a community and knowledge resource for submissives of all walks of life. She focuses on common sense advice and information to bring submission into reality for many.

About Submissive Guide

Submissive Guide is dedicated to helping submissives understand themselves and the service they wish to provide; from sexual to domestic, personal assistant to pain slut and everything in between.

Subguide prides itself on being the largest resource for submissives of all types, from novice to highly skilled. Since 2009, we've provided articles, ebooks, live chat, ecourses and more, all geared to helping submissives explore their personal journey in submission.

We invite you to come browse the extensive library of over 1500 articles or pick up a resource or two to add to your own collection.

https://submissiveguide.com

Submissive Reflection

Discover How to Nurture Your Submissive Mindset

Submissive Reflection: A Workbook is a perfect guide to helping you do that soul-searching and to really pinpoint where you are in your submissive journey right now. You'll gain understanding about how your personality, past relationships and inner code of ethics work together to define your submissive identity. Whether you have a partner or not, this workbook has the tools and knowledge to help you understand your place in submission.

You will adopt simple methods to take care of yourself and to nurture your submission through grooming and self-care tasks such as journaling, affirmations, and goal-setting.

Your submissive mindset is everything. And if you've lost your way, I want to help you find your way back. Let's discover it together!

https://submissiveguide.com/store/view-book/submissive-reflection

Made in the USA
Coppell, TX
10 January 2023